HOT TOPICS

OFFSHORE OIL DRILLING

Nick Hunter

Chicago, Illinois

www.heinemannraintree.com
Visit our website to find out
more information about
Heinemann-Raintree books.

To order:
☎ Phone 888-454-2279
🖳 Visit www.heinemannraintree.com
to browse our catalog and order online.

Edited by Adam Miller, Andrew Farrow, and
Jennifer Locke
Designed by Clare Webber and Steven Mead
Original illustrations © Capstone Global Library
Ltd.
Illustrated by Jeff Edwards
Picture research by Ruth Blair
Production by Eirian Griffiths
Originated by Capstone Global Library Ltd.
Printed and bound in China by Leo Paper
Group Ltd.

16 15 14 13 12
10 9 8 7 6 5 4 3 2 1

**Library of Congress Cataloging-in-
Publication Data**
Hunter, Nick.
  Off-shore oil drilling / Nick Hunter.—1st ed.
p. cm.—(Hot topics)
  Includes bibliographical references and
index.
  ISBN 978-1-4329-5176-4 (hc)
 1. Offshore oil industry. 2. Oil spills—
Cleanup. 3. Nature—Effect of human beings
on. I. Title. II. Series.
  HD9560.5.H866 2012
  622'.33819—dc22   2010044766

Acknowledgments
The author and publishers are grateful to the
following for permission to reproduce copyright
material: Alamy pp. **8** (© Ron Scott), **17**
(© Joe Baraban), **29** (© Accent Alaska.com),
33 (© Sergiy Serkyuk), **36** (© Imagestate
Media Partners Limited – Impact Photos),
41 (© Peter Titmuss), **42** (© Idealink
Photography), **43** (© Pascal Saez), **46** (©
Robert Harding Picture Library, Ltd.); Corbis
pp. **5** (© Martin Harvey), **13** (© Alain Nogues/
Sygma), **18** (© US Coast Guard/Handout), **20**
(© Xinhua/BP LIVE FEED/Xinhua Press), **21**
(© Julie Dermansky), **35** (© Bettmann), **46**
(© Julie Dermansky); Shutterstock pp. **6**
(© Rob Wilson), **11** (© Aguaviva), **25**
(© Photodynamic), **27** (© scoutingstock),
28 (© Becky Stares), **39** (© gallofoto), **49**
(© BlueOrange Studio).

Cover photograph of workers drilling for oil
reproduced with the permission of Corbis
(© Larry Lee Photography).

We would like to thank Kristen Kowalkowski
for her invaluable help in the preparation of
this book.

Every effort has been made to contact
copyright holders of any material reproduced
in this book. Any omissions will be rectified in
subsequent printings if notice is given to the
publisher.

CONTENTS

Some words are printed in bold, **like this**. You can find out what they mean by looking in the glossary.

BLACK GOLD

Finally, the oil had stopped leaking from the damaged well. Hundreds of feet below the surface of the Gulf of Mexico, the latest attempt to cap the leak seemed to be working. Oil workers, politicians, fishing communities, and others around the Gulf Coast and across the world held their breaths. They hoped that, after almost three months of oil pouring into the waters of the Gulf of Mexico, they could start to count the cost and repair the damage done by the world's biggest oil spill.

On April 20, 2010, an explosion on the Deepwater Horizon drilling rig, 52 miles (84 kilometers) off the coast of Louisiana killed 11 workers. As the rig burned and sank 5,000 feet (1,500 meters) to the sea bed, huge quantities of oil began to leak from the **oil well**. Oil drilling is nothing new to the people of the Gulf Coast—there are around 4,000 oil and gas rigs close to the U.S. coast. However, the Deepwater Horizon disaster showed many people the huge dangers that come with oil exploration.

Dangers of oil exploration

Even when things don't go wrong, finding and extracting oil can have a major impact on the environment. Drilling and transporting oil takes place in the oceans in wilderness areas affecting delicate **ecosystems**. Burning oil products in cars and power stations releases huge quantities of **carbon dioxide (CO_2)** that most scientists believe is responsible for major changes in our climate.

Our dependence on oil also has human costs. Eleven lives were lost in the Deepwater Horizon disaster, and drilling for oil and gas on isolated rigs far from the coast is always dangerous. The search for oil has tested technology and safety limits. This has led to growing concerns as the search for oil moves to more hard-to-reach places, including thousands of feet below the sea.

The reason why individuals and governments think that the huge risks of oil exploration are worth it is because of the importance of oil in the world today. Many of the world's biggest corporations are oil companies. The rulers of countries with big oil **reserves**, such as Saudi Arabia and Abu Dhabi, are some of the richest people in the world. Oil is so valuable that it is often known as "black gold."

> "The world does need the oil and the energy that is going to have to come from deep water production going forward."
> Steve Westwell, Chief of Staff, BP, June 2010 (Source: BBC News)

■ When oil spills into the sea, it can cause severe damage to **marine** and bird life.

A world without oil

To understand the importance of oil, you only have to consider what a world without oil would look like. We wouldn't be able to travel far in our world without oil. Most modern forms of transportation rely on oil. Trains and ships could be powered by other **fossil fuels** like coal and natural gas. Both these sources of energy are **non-renewable** and may run out one day. The roads would be rough too, without asphalt to make a smooth and weather-proof surface. Aircraft fuel also comes from oil.

Maybe we could run cars on electricity. Technology for electric cars is still developing. Some electricity is still produced using oil, although natural gas and coal are now used more widely. Oil is widely used to power home heating systems so we would have to find other ways of heating our houses.

■ Oil is a part of almost everything we do. In this game of basketball, oil was needed to make the ball, the shoes, the clothes, and the play area, as well as powering the cars or buses that got the players to the game.

OIL'S JOURNEY

When oil comes up from beneath the seabed it is known as **crude oil**. It contains a lot of different substances. This oil needs to be refined to be useful. It is sent through a network of pipelines on the seabed to refineries. At the **refinery**, the different substances are isolated by a process called **distillation**, which separates materials with different boiling points. **Petrochemical** products used to make everything from plastics to medicines only make up a small part of what we get from a barrel of crude oil.

Oil is also used in the manufacture of many artificial materials from plastics to paint. Look in every room of your house and you will find things made using oil, including clothes and shoes made from synthetic fabrics in your wardrobe; plastic bags, containers, and appliances in your kitchen; and many of the soaps, creams, and cosmetics in the bathroom.

The world we live in would be unrecognizable without oil. This is all the more amazing because oil has only been widely used in the last 150 years. It is also possible that one day we or our **descendants** will have to face a world without oil. Oil has formed over more than 100 million years so it is a non-renewable resource. This means that once it has been used, oil cannot be replaced.

Finding new oil reserves

No one quite knows how much oil there is left, but there is no immediate danger that it is about to run out. New reserves of oil are being found all the time. What we do know is that many reserves of oil that are relatively easy to access are being used up, and as oil becomes more difficult to access, we may find that it will become more difficult to supply the billions of **barrels** of oil that the world uses every day. Advances in technology mean that oil companies can drill for oil in places that would have been impossible a few years ago, such as deep beneath the ocean. As the Deepwater Horizon disaster shows, there is still much to find out about the risks of finding oil in the deep ocean.

WHAT IS OFFSHORE OIL DRILLING?

Drilling for oil beneath the seabed is nothing new. The first offshore drilling rig was constructed in the Gulf of Mexico in 1947. It operated in water that was just a few feet deep. During the decades that followed, thousands of offshore drilling rigs started operating around the world.

The coastal areas of the Gulf of Mexico became dotted with drilling rigs and oil platforms. By the 1980s, people were starting to say that they did not have the technology to find more oil in the area. Finding new oil would mean drilling in deep water, and most people thought that the limit for safe drilling was about 1,500 feet (450 meters) of water. However, in 1985 Shell, one of the world's biggest oil companies, began to drill at a depth of 3,218 feet (953 meters) and struck oil. Further deepwater discoveries followed and the race to find the oceans' oil was on.

■ Drilling oil wells in the deep waters of the Gulf of Mexico is difficult, dangerous, and very expensive.

Deep-sea oil drilling means drilling for oil at depths greater than 1,000 feet (305 meters). Many oil wells are much deeper than that. Shell's Perdido platform works in depths of around 9,600 feet (3 kilometers). Technology is constantly being developed to reach even greater depths. Often the oil itself is beneath many more thousands of feet of rock and salt below the seabed.

WHERE DOES OIL COME FROM?

Oil deposits do not normally happen in the middle of the deepest oceans but are found on **continental shelf** areas under deep water and rock. Oil and natural gas are formed over millions of years. They are made from plants and animals that decayed and were preserved in **sedimentary rock** close to Earth's surface. As new layers of rock were laid down, the decaying matter was heated and became crude oil and natural gas.

Oil and gas naturally rise to the surface through porous rocks that allow liquids to pass through them. For oil and gas to be useful, they have to be trapped beneath a layer of sedimentary rock that does not allow them to pass through it. If this trap is not present, the oil and gas will have seeped away. All these factors have to be in place for oil to be found on land or under the sea.

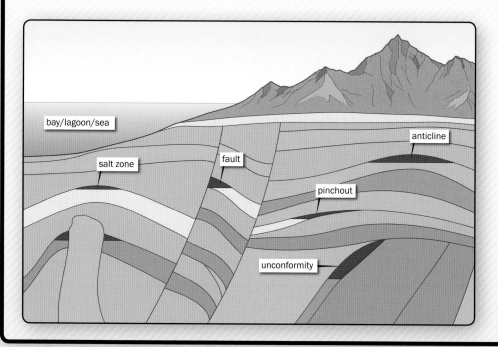

bay/lagoon/sea

anticline

salt zone

fault

pinchout

unconformity

Risks and rewards

The technical challenges and costs of looking for oil at these kinds of depths are enormous. Exploration teams need to be as sure as possible that they will find oil because drilling a test well in the deep ocean could cost $100 million. This is a lot of money even for a big oil corporation. They are prepared to take the risk because the rewards of success are huge.

Where does it happen?

The technology for deep-sea drilling has only developed in recent years but our hunger for oil is such that companies are already testing the technology to its limits in many locations around the world. Most of the early deep-sea drilling took place in the Gulf of Mexico and off the coasts of West Africa and Brazil.

Oil companies are planning to start drilling in many areas around the world, including near the Shetland Islands to the north of the United Kingdom. Some of the most controversial plans for deep-sea drilling are in the Arctic close to the coast of Greenland. The seas around Greenland are covered in ice for much of the year and the region is one of Earth's most precious habitats, with very little contact from humans. Environmental campaigners argue that the risk of major damage to this fragile region is too great.

Exploration close to the Falkland Islands in the South Atlantic is also hotly disputed. The islands are a British territory but are claimed by Argentina. The two countries fought a war over the islands in 1982 after Argentina invaded. Both countries are now claiming that any oil belongs to them.

World oil reserves

Although the number of deep-sea oil platforms has grown a lot in the last 20 years, they still make up only a tiny fraction of the world's oil production. The United States, which has the most deep-sea oil fields in production at present, is 13th on the list of countries with the biggest oil reserves. Oil reserves are an estimate of how much oil has been discovered but not yet used. New oil is being discovered all the time. Most of the countries with the biggest oil reserves are around the Persian Gulf, including Saudi Arabia, Iran, Iraq, and Kuwait. Saudi Arabia has ten times the oil reserves of the United States. Russia also has large oil reserves. Most of these reserves are accessible on land or in shallow coastal areas.

■ Many Arab states like Abu Dhabi have grown rich because of their huge oil reserves. Western countries want more control over their supply of oil.

THE GLOBAL OIL INDUSTRY

If deep-sea drilling is such a small part of world oil production compared to the massive reserves in the Middle East, why is it such a big deal? Part of the reason is explained by the shape of the global oil industry. Exxon-Mobil, Shell, and BP are some of the world's biggest oil companies. However, they only control about 10 percent of the world's oil reserves. Most of the rest is controlled by country-controlled oil companies of oil-rich countries like Saudi Arabia and Kuwait. Western oil companies and governments that do not control the huge oil reserves of countries like Saudi Arabia, Iran, and Russia are eager to find oil wherever they can. The biggest users of oil are the United States, China, and the European Union.

HOW DOES OFFSHORE DRILLING WORK?

The rewards of deep-sea drilling may be huge, but finding the oil is difficult and costly. The costs of drilling for oil in deep ocean mean that companies have to do a huge amount of research before deciding where to drill for oil. Advances in the technology of mapping the seabed and finding oil have been just as important as developments in drilling equipment in making deep-sea exploration possible. But, as we shall see, there are plenty of opportunities for things to go wrong.

Mapping the ocean floor

To find rock formations that may contain oil, the seabed has to be mapped in incredible detail. The difference between success and failure is huge. A few feet can sometimes mean the difference between a successful oil strike worth billions of dollars or a dry well that may cost around $100 million.

Creating a map of the seabed means doing a thorough **survey** that can pick up rock formations that might contain oil. This survey is carried out by several ships using **sonar** equipment that bounces sound waves off the seabed. These waves bounce off the seabed and are picked up by thousands of sensors pulled on long streamers behind the ships. This creates massive amounts of data that are processed by powerful computer systems to create a three-dimensional map, which also shows different layers below the seabed. **Geologists** use these maps to identify rock formations that may contain oil.

Once the company is sure they have found oil, they can think about drilling a test well. One oil industry expert has said that drilling for oil beneath thousands of feet of sea, rock, and salt is like drilling down through a two-story building filled with water and rock. In this example, the drill would be the width of a human hair, from a drilling platform as big as a matchbox, and trying to hit an oil reservoir the size of a coin below the building.

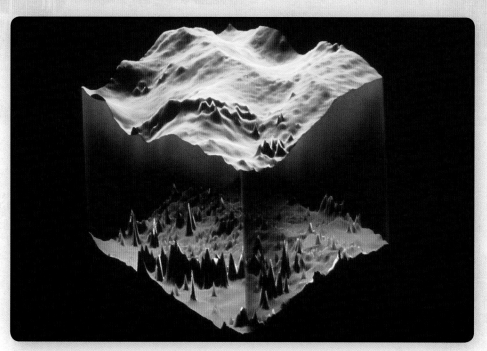

■ This is a computer-generated image of the seabed, made up from the astonishing amount of data collected by seismic survey ships. It may look confusing but geologists can tell the type and formation of rocks in great detail using this data.

THE COST OF SEARCHING FOR OIL IN THE GULF OF MEXICO

The Gulf of Mexico is where there has been most competition in deep-sea drilling. There are big costs for oil companies before they can find any oil.

- Oil companies buy leases from the government for different sections of the **continental shelf**, hoping they will be able to find oil. Different governments own areas of ocean around their coasts. Although oil companies do research, this is like buying a piece of land without knowing if you can build a house on it.

- Detailed **seismic** surveys and other studies of the seabed using several ships map the seabed. Robot submarines can also film the seabed.

- Drilling rigs that drill to huge depths can cost $600 million. Daily running costs are also huge at more than $200,000 per day.

If no oil is found, these costs are lost. It is important to work quickly but safely as exploratory costs are small compared to the costs and damage of a major accident.

Drilling the well

The latest drilling rigs are designed to drill to a depth of 40,000 feet (12,000 meters). The pipe used to drill the well, called the **drill string**, is made up of interlocking lengths of pipe. This can weigh 66 pounds (30 kg) per three feet so the overall weight needs a big rig to support it. The rigs themselves have to be kept in position. Sometimes they might be held in position by huge anchors, but the strong currents mean this is not practical in really deep water. Most deep-sea drilling rigs are held in place by **thrusters** that are linked to a GPS (Global Positioning System). Signals from satellites measure the position of the rig very accurately. If the rig moves, the thrusters activate to keep it in position.

The drilling lasts for several months. While the drill is boring through the rocks beneath the sea, the drilling team receives a lot of information from equipment at the bottom of the drill string. They find out about temperature, **pressure,** and whether there is resistance to electricity. This can indicate whether oil and gas are present, because they do not conduct electricity. A substance called drilling mud is pumped into the hole. This mud cools the drill bit and keeps the well under pressure. If the pressure is too low, outside forces will collapse the well. If pressure is too high, cracks in the wall of the well will widen and mud will escape.

The drilling team hopes to find oil that has been trapped underground for millions of years. The oil is contained in porous rock, a bit like a sponge, but harder. When the drill hits the oil reservoir, massive pressure from the rock above forces oil, gas, or both up the well, like soda escaping from a bottle, but more forceful.

Once the well is drilled, the oil will probably be taken out of the well by a huge oil platform, linked to many wells. People working on these platforms will not see oil gushing to the surface. It will usually be transported to oil terminals on the coast by a network of undersea pipes.

Drilling rigs

The Deepwater Horizon rig that exploded in 2010 causing the world's biggest oil disaster was a drilling rig. These rigs are used to drill wells and then move elsewhere. Huge drilling ships are also used. Giant oil platforms get the oil from the well to shore. In 2010, Shell's Perdido Spar production platform operated several wells in the Gulf of Mexico. At that time it was the world's deepest operating platform. The platform above the surface of the sea was as tall as the Eiffel Tower in Paris.

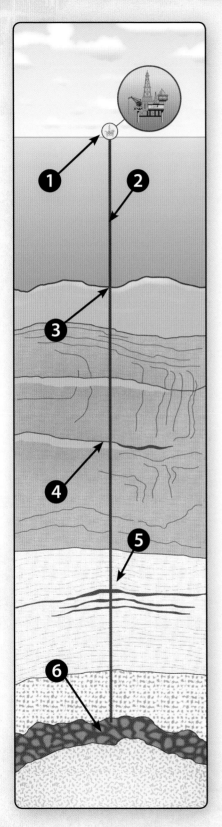

To extract oil, a rig will have to deal with freezing water, boiling oil, and seismic uncertainty.

1 At each corner of the drilling rig there are giant engines to keep things stable. When the ocean pulls one way, the thrusters push the other way.

2 The drill is made up of hundreds of linked pieces of iron, each one measuring 90 feet (27 meters). Buoyant sidings reduce the weight pressing on the rig.

3 The drill needs to enter the seafloor at exactly the right point, so that it does not hit an air pocket or a fault as it moves down. Boiling-hot oil comes out at the entry point and hits the freezing water. The underwater pipes that pump the oil back to shore must be heavily insulated.

4 The drill must cross a number of pressure zones. The drill could easily be knocked off course.

5 Bedrock mounds are formed by oil pushing upward. These mounds indicate oil is likely to be found there.

6 The oil is trapped in porous rock.

Safety concerns

Finding and drilling for oil is an incredibly complex process involving hundreds of people. There are things that could go wrong at each stage of the process. What are the risks and what is done to minimize those risks?

Deep water

Having detailed data before and during the drilling process makes deep-sea drilling possible but it cannot solve every problem. Drilling equipment can become stuck or broken. The deep ocean presents lots of problems, including the corrosive effect of salt water on metal rigs and drilling equipment. Equipment that is more than a mile below the surface is under extreme pressure. Pipes and equipment that work well in normal offshore drilling need to be much tougher to survive at these depths. Under extreme water pressure and at temperatures just above freezing, engineers encounter problems such as the fact that gases may become solid crystals, and this can disable equipment.

Much of the technology needed to extract oil is located below the surface. In some cases oil, gas, and water are separated by equipment on the seabed, so the oil and gas can be piped straight to the coast. Deep-sea wells are too deep for human divers to repair and check this equipment, so engineers rely on remote-controlled robots to maintain the incredibly complex network of pipes and **valves**. This means that when things go wrong, fixing a problem is more difficult.

Remote communities

The remoteness of the platforms themselves can also cause new risks. The most remote platforms are up to 200 miles (322 kilometers) from shore and are home to hundreds of workers. A major fire could be out of control long before the platform could be reached by boat. Oil companies say that safety is a major consideration and accidents are rare, but they can have a devastating impact on lives and the environment.

> "Our ability to manage risks hasn't caught up with our ability to explore and produce in deep water. The question now is, how are we going to protect against a **blowout** as well as all of the other associated risks offshore?"
> Edward C. Chow, Center for Strategic and International Studies
> (quoted in *The New York Times*, August 29, 2010)

Managing risks

Managing risk is very important for large projects such as drilling an oil well. Companies need to understand what can go wrong and have plans in place. Ways of dealing with risks include:

- Reduce the risk, by having safety and recovery plans in place.
- Eliminate the risks by doing something differently such as not drilling during the hurricane season.
- Accept a risk and have plans in place to deal with the effects, such as dealing with a massive oil spill.

WEATHER WARNING

Huge oil platforms in the open ocean have to deal with the full force of nature. Hurricanes are storms in which the wind blows at more than 74 miles per hour (119 kilometers per hour). They affect tropical regions including the Gulf of Mexico and East Asia. In Asia, these storms are called typhoons. When a hurricane is expected, oil production has to be shut down and platforms evacuated. Even the biggest oil platforms can be damaged by hurricanes, as well as the pipelines that bring the oil to the shore.

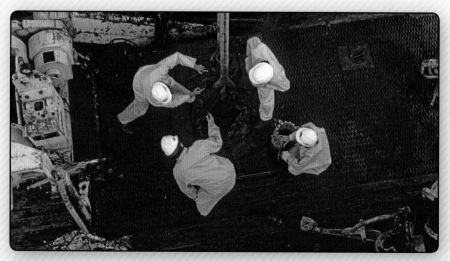

■ BP's Thunder Horse platform was damaged by Hurricane Katrina.

THE DEEPWATER HORIZON OIL SPILL

The Deepwater Horizon drilling rig was one of the most advanced rigs around. In September 2009, it had set a record for the deepest well when it had drilled to a depth of 35,055 feet (10,685 meters). By April 20, drilling of a new well in the Mississippi Canyon area of the Gulf of Mexico was almost finished. The top of the well was about 5,000 feet (1,500 meters) below the surface of the Gulf of Mexico. The cement and metal casing needed to stop the well from collapsing was in place. The team was due to cap the well with concrete until it was ready to be used. The oil well was owned by the giant oil company BP.

Disaster strikes

At around 9:30 p.m. on April 20, drilling mud and seawater began to gush out of the well and up the drill string. Soon after, the rig was shaken by a massive explosion as gas reached the surface. The explosion killed 11 people and injured many others. More than 100 people were evacuated by air and sea as the fire burned out of control. After burning for 36 hours, the Deepwater Horizon sank.

■ Fire-fighting boats tried desperately to extinguish the fire on the Deepwater Horizon rig.

Almost a mile below, oil began to leak into the ocean from the ruptured well. Investigators were unsure how much oil was leaking. After a few days it became clear that thousands of gallons of oil were gushing from the well. It could have a massive impact on the ocean environment, the coast, and the lives of thousands of people. Everyone from fishermen to seaside hotel owners depended on the waters and beaches of the Gulf Coast to make their living.

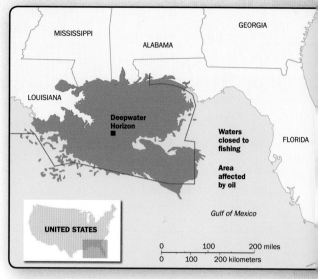

This map shows the area affected by the Deepwater Horizon spill.

WHAT WENT WRONG?

According to the initial report by BP, the first of many investigations, the disaster on the Deepwater Horizon was caused by a number of different things.

- Problems with the cement lining meant that gas could escape into the well. The crew on the rig failed to pick up the problem and relaxed the pressure in the well.
- A huge piece of machinery fitted to the top of the well, called a blowout preventer, should have stopped the gas from reaching the surface, but it failed to work.
- Fire and safety procedures on the rig were not followed. A report before the disaster found concerns about safety and maintenance.

Two other companies were involved in the accident. Transocean owned the oil rig and Halliburton cemented the well. They said that the well was badly designed and safety issues were ignored by BP to save costs.

Capping the well

The desperate struggle to stop the gushing oil continued until the flow was finally stopped on July 15, 2010 (see box). As many attempts to stop the flow failed, officials and the media began to

ask whether there were proper plans in place for dealing with deep-sea oil disasters. The plan that BP had prepared before drilling the well had said that an accident at the well that would lead to a major oil spill was "unlikely."

By the time the Deepwater Horizon oil spill was stopped almost three months after it started, it had become the worst accidental oil spill in history. Why was it so bad and so difficult to stop? As the table on page 22 shows, the world's worst oil spills have either come from leaking oil wells or from oil tankers being wrecked and spilling their contents into the sea. Oil wells are so dangerous because they can continue to leak for many months if they aren't stopped. The depth of the well made it much more difficult to cap. Many of the techniques and equipment used had never been tried at such a great depth.

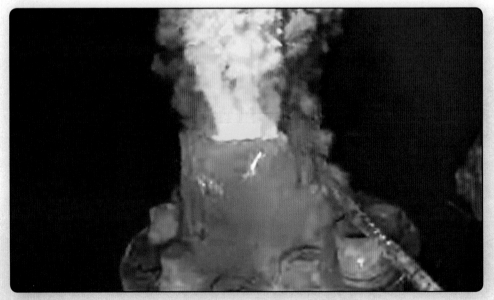

■ Estimates of how much oil was gushing from the well increased as the disaster unfolded.

Oil booms in Mobile Bay, Alabama, were installed to protect the inner waterways from the oil that had made its way to the coast.

TIMELINE OF THE DISASTER

April 20, 2010 – Explosion and fire on the Deepwater Horizon drilling rig. The rig sinks on April 22.

April 30 – Oil begins to wash ashore in fragile Louisiana **wetlands**.

May 8 – BP tries to contain the leak using a metal box on top of it. Officials say that the leak could be up to 5,000 barrels per day.

May 26 – BP unsuccessfully tries to stop oil flow with heavy drilling mud. The mud is designed to overcome the pressure of the rising oil, forcing it back down the well.

June 4 – BP places a cap on the well. A few days later, BP says they are collecting 15,800 barrels per day by this method. The size of the spill is now estimated at 40,000 barrels per day.

June 15 – President Obama says he will "make BP pay" for the disaster.

July 15 – BP fits a new cap to the well which stops the oil flowing.

August 3 – U.S. government says the disaster is the world's biggest oil spill with 4.9 million barrels of oil leaking. About 800,000 barrels were captured by the clean-up effort.

August 5 – U.S. coastguard says that the ruptured oil well poses no further risk to the environment. The well is finally declared "effectively dead" when it is sealed with concrete on September 19.

The clean-up

The Deepwater Horizon oil disaster had a huge impact on the people and the environment of the Gulf of Mexico. Many of the people working on the clean-up were from the fishing communities around the coast. These people make their living by fishing in the Gulf. Fishing was banned across a huge area because of fears that fish could be **contaminated** with oil. Businesses that rely on tourism were also affected along a huge stretch of coastline from Florida to Louisiana. People working for and supporting the oil industry, from helicopter pilots to caterers for platforms, were also affected as new drilling was put on hold.

In August 2010, the U.S. National Ocean and Atmospheric Administration (NOAA) said that the majority of oil was gone from the area. Some oil had been captured and piped up to vessels on the surface. The rest had evaporated, been burnt on the surface of the ocean, or broken down by **dispersants**. Scientists are concerned that oil is still present in huge underwater plumes that will be around for years. Bacteria break down this oil but as they do so, they use oxygen in the water which means that fish and other marine mammals are less able to survive.

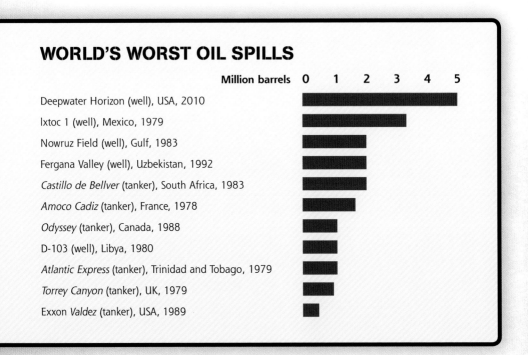

WORLD'S WORST OIL SPILLS

	Million barrels 0 1 2 3 4 5
Deepwater Horizon (well), USA, 2010	
Ixtoc 1 (well), Mexico, 1979	
Nowruz Field (well), Gulf, 1983	
Fergana Valley (well), Uzbekistan, 1992	
Castillo de Bellver (tanker), South Africa, 1983	
Amoco Cadiz (tanker), France, 1978	
Odyssey (tanker), Canada, 1988	
D-103 (well), Libya, 1980	
Atlantic Express (tanker), Trinidad and Tobago, 1979	
Torrey Canyon (tanker), UK, 1979	
Exxon Valdez (tanker), USA, 1989	

Worse than the oil?

Dispersants are chemicals that break up oil into smaller droplets so it can be broken down by oil-eating **micro-organisms**. Millions of gallons were used in cleaning up the oil spill. Many scientists believe that dispersants can do as much damage to marine life as the oil itself, although the dispersants can help to break up the oil before it reaches the coastline to break up oil slicks. In the Deepwater Horizon spill, they were also used underwater to break up oil before it reached the surface. There is evidence that coral is more damaged by dispersants than it is by oil itself. Using the dispersants underwater could mean long-term damage to coral reefs in the Gulf.

Even though much of the oil was dispersed, there was still thought to be more than one million barrels of oil that could be a danger to the coast and marine life. The short-term effects of the spill are much clearer than long-term effects that may take many years to become clear. The Mexican Ixtoc 1 disaster in 1979 was the world's worst oil accident until 2010.

Louisiana wetlands

Oil reached the wetlands on the Louisiana coast just a few days after the disaster began and by May the wetlands were clogged with sheets of oil. The oil here will have a short–term impact, killing many birds and turtles as they become covered in oil, but also a long-term impact on such an important environment.

The impact on fish further out in the Gulf will only become clear over many years. Those who earn their living from fishing are waiting anxiously to see what effect there may be on fish such as tuna and shrimp that are caught in the Gulf.

The Deepwater Horizon disaster has shaken the confidence of governments and the general public in deep-sea drilling. The US government introduced restrictions on new deep-sea drilling and will require companies to think much more about the environmental impact of their activities in future.

ENVIRONMENTAL IMPACT

The Deepwater Horizon disaster shows that spills from deep-sea drilling can be much more difficult to stop than other types of oil disasters. Many governments have started to think about the effect that similar disasters could have on their own marine environment.

Oil in the environment

As oil is released into the sea, it floats to the surface and forms a layer on top of the water. This is known as an oil slick and it spreads where the wind and currents take it. The oil coats all it touches, including birds and other marine animals. Birds are poisoned by oil as they try to clean their feathers. Oil affects the entire food supply in a marine environment as wetland plants and other food sources, such as smaller fish, become coated with oil.

Oil remains in the environment for a long time. It evaporates and breaks down more quickly in warmer than in colder seas. Areas currently being considered for deep-sea exploration are very cold, including the Arctic. Although the 1989 spill from the Exxon *Valdez* in Alaska involved less oil than the Deepwater Horizon disaster, the oil lasted longer and more seabirds were affected because the oil dispersed slowly in the cold sea. Also, the accident happened near the coast, so oil couldn't be dispersed before it coated the shore.

Impact of deep-sea oil exploration

Even when oil exploration is successful, it can have a major impact on the environment. Sound waves used in seismic surveys of the seabed can affect marine life, including whales' communication with each other and navigation. Oil drilling and pipelines can also have a huge impact on the seabed.

Drilling for oil also produces other hazardous materials, like water containing substances that are poisonous to wildlife. Human communities can also be damaged by the engineering and support services that the industry brings to sometimes isolated coastlines. These effects need to be balanced against the economic benefits and jobs that the oil industry brings to these areas.

CASE STUDY

Oil and Antarctica

One of the few places on Earth that has not yet been affected by the quest for oil is Antarctica. Antarctica is protected by a treaty that stops any country from oil exploration on the continent or in the seas around it until at least 2048. The continent is believed to have large oil reserves. In the 1980s, as drilling technology developed, companies started to look at the possibility of oil exploration in the seas around Antarctica. It was agreed that Antarctica's fragile and almost untouched ecosystem was too important to be damaged by oil exploration.

Making choices

International agreements have preserved Antarctica's delicate ecosystem up to now, but will this continue? Is protecting this environment more important than finding the oil needed for transportation and heating? What will happen if the price of oil and related products rises so the environment can be protected?

Oil exploration on land

Although deep-sea oil exploration can harm the environment, looking for oil on land can have an even bigger impact. Oil drilling on land has a direct effect on habitats for plants and animals. It can also have a big impact on people.

We know that oil companies are looking for oil in deeper waters where the oil is more difficult to access and the risks are greater. This is because easier sources of oil are drying up. The same thing is happening with attempts to find oil on land. Oil companies and others would like to drill for oil in places like the Arctic National Wildlife Refuge (see box), but many environmental campaigners believe this is impossible without doing huge damage.

Transporting oil

Many oil disasters have been caused by the transportation of oil. Oil tankers are huge ships that can carry more than a million barrels of oil. Many of the world's worst oil disasters have been tanker accidents. One of the arguments for more deep-sea drilling closer to countries that use a lot of oil, like the United States and European Union countries, is that less oil will have to come from the Middle East in tankers. Oil from offshore drilling is normally brought ashore through a network of pipelines.

Pipeline problems

However, pipelines are not a perfect solution. In 2006, more than 6,000 barrels of oil leaked from pipelines operated by BP that had become corroded. Although this was a tiny spill compared to many oil well and tanker disasters, the oil leaked into the fragile environment of Alaska. There are thousands of miles of pipelines beneath the Gulf of Mexico. Deep-sea oil wells need to be linked to these pipelines using robot submarines that lay pipes across the seabed and link them up to existing pipelines. Pipelines deep in the ocean need to withstand huge pressures. Materials and connections that are too weak can break, allowing oil to spill into the ocean. As well as corrosion, pipelines could be attacked or damaged by natural disasters like earthquakes.

ARCTIC NATIONAL WILDLIFE REFUGE

The Arctic National Wildlife Refuge (ANWR) is a huge area of wilderness on the north coast of Alaska, which is part of the United States. It is home to many species of marine and land animals and birds. The U.S. Geological Survey has estimated that there are probably more than 10 billion barrels of oil beneath this protected area. Environmental campaigners believe that drilling for oil in the ANWR would affect the number of species in the region. They pointed out that although drilling might affect only a small area, workers would need to live in the area and roads and pipelines would need to be built. A 2003 report on Alaska's oil industry found that 596 miles (959 kilometers) of road had been built in the north Alaskan wilderness as part of oil exploration in the area. Although many people are in favor of drilling in the ANWR, this area has so far been preserved.

■ If oil tankers run aground, oil can be released directly on to the coast. When the Exxon *Valdez* ran aground in Alaska in 1989, as many as 600,000 seabirds died. This was a much higher figure than in the Deepwater Horizon disaster, which happened farther out at sea.

Climate change

As well as the environmental impact of drilling for oil deep in the oceans and the problems of transporting it safely, using oil and gas also has a big impact on the environment. Most oil is burned to power vehicles like cars and airplanes. This releases so-called "**greenhouse gases**," including carbon dioxide (CO_2). Most scientists believe that our use of oil and other fossil fuels is causing Earth's climate to heat up as more CO_2 is released into the atmosphere. If climate change continues, it will have a huge impact on all of us. Scientists predict that sea levels will rise as huge sheets of ice in the Arctic and Antarctic start to melt. Hot regions will get hotter and deserts will spread, meaning there will be less fertile land to grow food.

Although we know we need to reduce our reliance on oil, the total amount of oil used around the world has increased from just over 66 million barrels per day in 1990 to 84 million barrels per day in 2009. This is one major reason why oil companies and others argue that we need to find new sources of oil, even in places where it is difficult and expensive to get to. Otherwise, oil prices will continue to rise, which is usually very unpopular.

■ Some people argue that money should be invested in alternatives to oil and other fossil fuels, like this wind farm, rather than on drilling technology.

■ Alaska is home to a huge variety of wildlife. Is oil more important than these wild places?

DEBATE

IS THE ENVIRONMENT MORE IMPORTANT THAN BEING ABLE TO ACCESS OIL?

Oil companies, governments, and sometimes local people, are looking for new areas to drill for oil. Some people think we should use whatever oil is available while others think protecting the environment is important.

Arguments for:

- Once wild places have been damaged by oil exploration, they are lost forever. Rare species of animals and plants may never recover.

- We damage the environment when we use oil as we are taking it out of the ground. We should be spending the money to find oil in deep oceans and wild places or on finding alternatives to oil.

- When things go wrong in oil exploration, it can do huge damage to environments such as oceans, and the plants and animals that live there.

Arguments against:

- Oil is so important to our lives; we should use all available sources.

- As long as governments make sure that oil companies don't damage the environment more than necessary, and impose tough penalties for damage caused, we can get the oil we need.

- Oil exploration can bring wealth to areas where people are living in **poverty** or where there are few opportunities to work.

IS OFFSHORE DRILLING NECESSARY?

Drilling for oil in deep offshore waters is hugely expensive. The risks are also very great. As explorers look for new sources of oil, they will continue to test the limits of technology in extreme environments. Given the risks and danger of deep-sea exploration, is it really necessary?

Thirst for oil

Supporters of deep-sea drilling argue that our thirst for oil is so great that we need to explore all possible ways of finding more oil, even if they may be very difficult. The amount of oil used around the world has been increasing fairly steadily for many years. Many countries, including the United States, saw their use of oil fall in 2008 and 2009 because of difficult economic conditions. The United States still uses more than 20 percent of all the oil used world-wide. However, China, which is the biggest user of oil after the United States and the European Union, saw its use of oil almost double in the 10 years to 2009. India has also seen a big growth in its use of oil. Industrialization and more oil being used in **developing countries** mean that our oil use continues to grow and is not likely to fall without drastic action.

At the same time, there is less new oil being discovered than there was in the past. Oil is a non-renewable resource and oil fields will not go on providing oil forever. Many oil fields have started to produce less oil, including some of the biggest ones in countries with the most oil, such as Kuwait and Saudi Arabia. As the world uses more than 30 billion barrels of oil every year, oil companies need to keep finding new reserves of oil.

Even without new oil being discovered, there are enough known oil reserves to last about 50 years if we continue to use oil at the same rate. So, what's the problem? The problem is that experts now think we are close to the peak of how much oil we can produce.

WILL DEEP-SEA DRILLING GIVE US ENOUGH OIL?

Only a very small part of the world's oil reserves come from deep-sea drilling. In 2008, deepwater oil only made up about 2 percent of world oil reserves. However, if we remember that about 75 percent of the oil we know about is beneath the deserts of the Middle East, then deep-sea oil makes up a much bigger part of the oil in the rest of the world. Although the growth of deep-sea oil exploration has slowed due to the Deepwater Horizon disaster, its importance is likely to grow in the future.

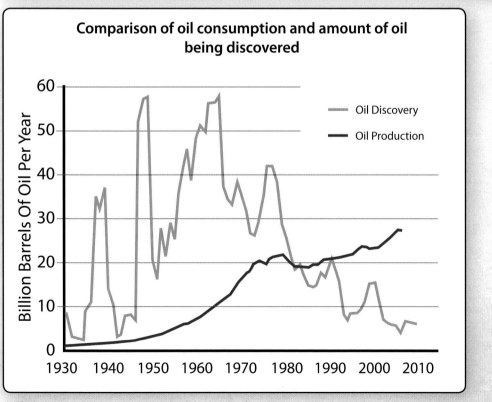

Comparison of oil consumption and amount of oil being discovered

■ If oil use continues to rise, more oil will have to be found to meet the demand.

Oil reserves include some oil that is more difficult to reach and as oil fields get older, it costs more to extract each barrel of oil. As oil is removed from an oil field, the remaining oil is under less pressure so does not come to the surface as quickly. It's a bit like wringing out a wet cloth—it's easy to get the first drops of water out but it gets more and more difficult. This will be a big problem if demand for oil keeps increasing, as oil prices will start to rise.

Other sources of oil

There are fewer easy sources of oil than there have been in the past. Areas like the North Sea, which has been able to provide much of the United Kingdom's energy needs, and oil fields in Texas are now what is known as "mature," meaning that there is less oil coming from them than in the past, and it is more difficult to get to. Deep-sea oil is not the only source of oil that is being investigated by oil companies. Are other sources of oil any better?

Tar sands

Tar sands, also called oil sands, are one possible solution to our thirst for oil. There are large areas of tar sands in Alberta, Canada and in northern United States including North Dakota. Many of these tar sands are close to the surface. They are made of sand and clay mixed with bitumen, an almost solid substance that is a form of crude oil.

In order to be made into liquid oil that can be refined, tar sands require huge amounts of energy, from either natural gas or nuclear sources. They also require a lot of water, in areas that have low rainfall. It takes 2 tons (1.8 tonnes) of tar sand to make one barrel of crude oil. People are concerned about the environmental damage from tar sands and the energy costs of turning them into usable crude oil. The energy used to convert the bitumen to liquid oil means that tar sands are an even bigger contributor to greenhouse gases than other forms of oil. If nuclear energy was used, this would reduce the amount of greenhouse gases produced but may create other safety issues. Despite all these problems, the desperation for new sources of oil means that oil from tar sands in Canada is now the United States' largest source of **imported** oil. Oil production from tar sands is a growing slice of Canada's CO_2 emissions.

Just like deep-sea oil drilling, other alternative sources of oil present major risks and environmental challenges. The biggest reserves of oil are still in the Middle East. Why are governments and oil companies so desperate to find other sources of oil?

NORTH SEA OIL

The North Sea is the stretch of water between Great Britain and mainland Europe. Since oil was discovered in the North Sea in the 1960s, it has provided much of the oil used by the United Kingdom and other European countries including Norway. The North Sea is a good example of a declining, or "mature," area for oil exploration. Oil production peaked in the mid 1990s and has been declining steadily since. Although North Sea oil production is based on offshore oil platforms, up to now they have been in relatively shallow water. Oil companies claim to have found new oil fields close to the United Kingdom but this will mean drilling in deep water close to the Shetland Islands.

■ Pumpjacks are a familiar sight in Texas, but oil is beginning to run dry.

POLITICS AND OIL SECURITY

Most of the countries that use the most oil, including the USA, countries of the European Union, China, and Japan are not countries with huge oil reserves. They have to import much of the oil they use. Over the years, the need to import oil has increased as these countries have used more oil and their own oil production has declined in some cases.

Most of the world's largest oil **exporting** countries are part of a group called **OPEC (Organization of Petroleum Exporting Countries)**. OPEC currently has 12 members. The countries of OPEC account for about 75 percent of the world's known oil reserves. The organization's aim is to maintain stable oil prices by co-ordinating how much oil they produce.

Oil prices

Many of the large oil-producing countries within OPEC manage oil production through country-owned companies rather than working with multinational oil companies such as Exxon, Shell, and BP. These countries can change the amount of oil they produce to influence the global price of oil. This affects economies in the rest of the world. Drivers have to pay more for the fuel that goes into cars and trucks. It increases the cost of transporting and delivering goods to shops and customers so prices of many goods and services rise.

Political instability

Countries that import a lot of oil from the Middle East are also concerned about political instability in the region. Iran has the world's second largest oil reserves. The country also has a government that is unfriendly to many Western countries. Western governments including the United States and the United Kingdom accuse Iran of helping **terrorists** and other conflicts across the Middle East.

IS THE AGE OF CHEAP OIL OVER?

Oil is sold by traders around the world. The price goes up and down depending on how much demand there is for oil. Those who use oil, such as businesses and car drivers, want the price to be as low as possible. Those who supply oil want prices to be higher, but not so high that people will start to consider alternatives to using oil. Many people believe that there are several reasons why the price of oil is likely to rise in the future.

- Oil production will begin to decline, meaning that there will be more demand and less supply.
- New developments, including deep-sea drilling, require more investment. It will not be worthwhile for companies to look for this oil if prices are too low.
- Demand will continue to increase from growing industrial nations such as China, as well as developing countries.

If supply is declining or becoming more expensive and demand is increasing that is a recipe for rising oil prices.

■ In 1973, OPEC members increased oil prices. They also cut supply to countries that were supporting Israel in the Yom Kippur War against Arab states Egypt and Syria. High prices and shortages of oil gave many countries a taste of the dangers of relying on imported oil.

■ When the U.S. and her allies invaded Iraq in 2003, oil wells were set on fire by the Iraqi regime. Problems like this could disrupt oil supplies in future.

Iraq also has some of the world's biggest oil reserves. Iraq has been involved in a number of wars in the region, including the recent invasion by the United States and her **allies** in 2003.

Unstable governments and anti-Western feeling in these countries mean that there is a possibility that oil supplies could be interrupted at some point in the future. Any interruption in supply could cause major problems for countries that import a lot of oil.

Russia is the leading producer of oil and exports it to many countries. Russia is also the world's largest supplier of natural gas and has been known to turn off supplies of gas to neighbors like Ukraine due to political disputes.

Competition for oil

Another major factor in the global supply of oil is growing competition for oil supplies. China, India, and Brazil all have growing demands for oil. This competition for oil gives more power to countries that have their own oil, as global oil production declines in the decades to come.

Many governments are concerned about political risks to the global oil supply resulting in countries being keen to find and control their own oil reserves. Oil companies also want to find new supplies of oil as they are excluded from many of the Middle Eastern oil companies. Although there are big risks in deep-sea oil drilling, many governments feel that the risks of not exploiting their own oil reserves are even greater if the price of oil imports is too high or conflict interrupts the supply of oil.

DEBATE

IS IT BETTER TO FIND NEW SOURCES OF OIL OR RELY ON OIL FROM OTHER COUNTRIES?

Many oil companies and governments that import most of their oil think it is better to find new sources of oil. Look at both sides of the debate and decide what you think.

Arguments for:

- The main sources of oil are politically unstable and supply of oil could be disrupted. Deep-sea drilling reduces this risk.
- Competition for oil supplies from countries like China and India will mean higher prices for oil world-wide.
- Even if the supply of oil from the Middle East is not disrupted, it will start to run out in the future so we need to keep finding new sources of oil. It can take a long time to find new sources, and develop new technologies, so we need to be doing it now.

Arguments against:

- Deep-sea oil exploration and other new sources of oil are much more expensive than importing oil from the Middle East.
- Up to now, new sources of oil can only meet a small amount of the demand for oil so countries like the United States will always need to import much of their oil.
- Countries looking for new sources of oil run the risk of doing serious damage to their local environment, such as in the Deepwater Horizon disaster.
- If we are to combat climate change, we need to find alternatives to oil rather than different sources of oil.

WHAT ARE THE ALTERNATIVES?

Although there are many reasons why deep-sea drilling is desirable for countries that do not want to rely on imported oil, we have seen that there are many drawbacks and issues with the search for oil reserves beneath the ocean floor. Can we keep the lifestyle we are used to, while reducing our reliance on oil?

We can reduce our reliance on oil by reducing its use in cars, plastics, and all the other places we use oil. Around half of the oil we use is made into gasoline for cars. In fact, most of each barrel of oil is used for transportation if we include diesel for buses, jet fuel, and heavy oil used to power ships. There are many ways to reduce the oil we use for transportation. One way is by driving cars that use less fuel. Some large SUVs or four-wheel-drive vehicles use 1 gallon (4.5 liters) of gasoline for every 10 miles they travel. By contrast, hybrid cars can do 60 miles for every gallon they use. These cars use an electric motor as well as an engine that burns gasoline to reduce how much fuel they use. Although many public transportation systems use oil, they are using less oil per passenger than cars, which will often only contain one person.

OIL AND DEVELOPING COUNTRIES

One of the problems in reducing oil use is being fair to developing countries. The whole of Africa uses less oil than the United Kingdom and France combined and around one-sixth of the oil used by the United States. However, oil use in developing countries is growing as they become more industrialized. Is it fair to ask developing countries to reduce how much oil they use? After all, climate change has been caused by carbon emissions from the richest countries of the world. Developing countries ask why they should be denied the opportunity to develop their economies and improve living standards for their peoples in the same way.

■ More recycling of oil-based products like plastics would mean that we would need less oil. Also, using less plastic means the need for less recyling.

Food miles

Oil is also used in ships and aircraft to transport goods. Many of the foods and other goods we buy are imported from other countries such as China. We can reduce the amount of oil we use by choosing to buy things made or grown closer to home. This will also help local businesses. There are many other ways we can save oil, such as by reusing and recycling plastic goods.

International agreements

Although many of us can try to reduce our own use of oil, it is difficult to see the impact of this without businesses and individuals across the world reducing the amount of oil they use. There have been a number of international agreements that have tried to reduce **emissions** of carbon, in the form of carbon dioxide. In the Kyoto Protocol of 1997, countries agreed on targets for reducing carbon emissions. The agreement has been only partially successful, not least because the United States rejected it, complaining that it did not include lower emissions targets for developing countries, including rapidly growing economies such as India and China.

International agreements to reduce carbon emissions should force countries to reduce their use of oil, but oil and other fossil fuels are likely to be with us for some time to come. Like oil, natural gas and coal are non-renewable fuels and will run out eventually.

Using other fossil fuels

Natural gas emits a third less carbon dioxide than oil for the same amount of energy, and it is a better alternative to oil for some uses. However, there are many of the same issues around gas having to be imported from countries like Russia and Iran. Russia's country-controlled gas company Gazprom controls about one-fifth of the world's gas reserves and controls much of the supply of gas to the European Union.

Many of the gas reserves of countries like the United States and United Kingdom are, like oil, deep beneath the ocean floor. This means that they are expensive to find and extract, but the risk of devastating pollution from offshore drilling is much smaller than it is for crude oil because gas will evaporate into the atmosphere if it is released. The main risk from gas is that large quantities can explode. As the Deepwater Horizon disaster shows, releasing natural gas can be a major hazard when drilling for oil beneath the sea.

Coal is still relatively plentiful but less efficient than other fossil fuels. It is still used to generate electricity but it has fewer uses and creates more pollution than oil. There are ways of reducing the carbon released by fossil fuels, either by capturing the carbon when it is released or by treating the fuel before it is burned to reduce much of the carbon.

Nuclear power

Nuclear power releases energy by fission or the breaking down of large atoms of substances like uranium. Opponents argue that it is not safe after a number of accidents caused the release of dangerous radioactive material. Many countries are looking again at nuclear power as a source of energy. Nuclear power can generate the large amounts of electricity necessary to replace fossil fuels in power stations. However, many people still have concerns about the problem of disposing of hazardous radioactive fuel. They point out that if radiation is released in the environment, its effects are not easily visible but are just as dangerous as a major oil spill.

BIOFUELS

Biofuels are any plants that can be used to provide fuel. It particularly refers to ethanol and bio-diesel made from processing plants. Biofuels are one energy source that may replace some of the use of oil in cars. They can be mixed with gasoline to produce fuels that emit fewer **greenhouse gases**. Plants for biofuels also absorb carbon dioxide while they are growing, as do all plants. The main drawbacks with biofuels are that space is needed to grow them, which could damage wildlife habitats or reduce the amount of space we have to grow food. **Environmentalists** believe that we should focus our efforts on sources of energy that do not emit greenhouse gases.

■ About one-fifth of every barrel of oil is used for aircraft fuel. One day, biofuels may make up part of this fuel. This plane is powered by biofuels.

Gas, nuclear power, and even biofuels can all reduce our reliance on oil to some extent. However, they all have drawbacks, whether in the carbon emissions of gas, or the hazardous waste that is a result of nuclear power.

Renewable energy

There are many sources of energy in nature that can be used to generate electricity. Hydro-electricity relies on the energy created by water flowing downhill, or wave and tidal forces. Geothermal energy uses the heat below Earth's surface to generate power. Other sources of energy include the wind and solar energy. These energy sources are totally **renewable** but huge areas would have to be covered with wind turbines or solar panels to make up for the energy we get from oil. Compared to oil, these sources of energy provide a very small amount of the energy we use.

Many oil companies have also looked at alternatives to oil. Alongside their attempts to find new sources of oil, they have put money into renewable sources of energy. In recent years, companies like Shell and Exxon Mobil have invested in biofuels. However, investments in renewable energy have been a tiny part of what the oil companies spend. Between 2004 and 2009, According to *The New York Times*, Shell said it had spent $1.7 billion on renewable energy sources. This is dwarfed by the $87 billion the company spent on oil and gas projects over the same period.

Environmental campaigners claim that some oil companies, such as Exxon Mobil, have continued to fund organizations that deny that burning fossil fuels is causing climate change.

Whatever we think about the prospects for renewable energy in the long term, it seems as though, for the foreseeable future, new sources of oil will be important.

■ Solar powered cars look exciting but they are not a realistic replacement for oil-powered cars at present.

■ These turbines are designed to capture wave energy. Will renewable energy sources ever be able to replace oil?

DEBATE

ARE THERE REALISTIC ALTERNATIVES TO DRILLING IN DEEP WATER FOR OIL?

Do you think there are any fuels that could replace oil, or reduce our reliance on it so we don't have to keep drilling for oil in the ocean?

Arguments for:

- There are other sources of energy that will do less environmental damage than oil, such as gas, biofuels, and nuclear energy.
- Money spent on deep-sea exploration could be spent on reducing our use of oil and developing renewable alternatives.
- Continuing use of oil and other fossil fuels is not an option if we want to combat climate change—alternatives need to be found.

Arguments against:

- Oil consumption is still increasing and is likely to increase for years to come so we should continue to investigate all sources of oil.
- Other fossil fuels will not provide a real alternative and will not contribute to combating climate change.
- Nuclear and renewable sources of energy will not be able to make up the difference if oil production falls.
- Biofuels are only a partial solution and will take up huge areas of land that are needed for other things.

CONTROLLING "BIG OIL"

Big oil companies are massive multinational corporations. They operate in many different locations around the world. Many campaigners believe that big oil companies are out of control. Their argument is that, because they are so big and oil is such an essential resource, the companies can have too much influence on governments. Critics point to the fact that the lure of oil for governments and companies leads to human rights abuses in some of the world's poorest countries, such as in West Africa.

Companies argue that they are responsible to their customers and governments. They employ thousands of people and provide a resource that businesses and individuals need every day. They argue that they have to be big because small companies could not undertake the complicated work involved. They make big profits but this means they can afford to invest in risky oil exploration in deep waters. If the companies don't find oil, they will lose a lot of money.

ALTERNATIVES TO BIG OIL COMPANIES

Multinational oil companies are certainly not perfect. However, they do have to follow the laws of national governments around the world and report back to their shareholders, who own the company. Other sources of oil may be even less accountable. Oil companies in many Middle Eastern countries are owned by the state. Countries like Libya and Saudi Arabia are not democracies and are accused of human rights abuses and restricting the freedom of the media to criticize governments and the oil industry. Western oil companies and countries that import oil may turn a blind eye to these issues when they buy oil from these countries.

Safety and the environment

Critics of big oil companies claim that they do not pay enough attention to the safety of workers and the environment that is affected by accidents and spills. A report by the U.S. National Wildlife Federation found that there were 1,440 offshore leaks and other accidents around the United States between 2001 and 2007, which caused 41 deaths and more than 300 injuries. Offshore drilling was not necessarily less safe—during the same period, 161 people died in pipeline and refinery accidents on land. Many of those who died in onshore incidents were not connected to the oil industry at all, such as the 12 innocent passers-by killed when a pipeline exploded in New Mexico in 2000.

As well as the people killed and injured in oil accidents, many of these incidents caused major environmental damage. At the same time as the Deepwater Horizon disaster was making headlines around the world, China was also dealing with its worst-ever oil disaster after an explosion at an oil refinery led to an oil spill along the coast. Deepwater Horizon was not even the only oil spill in the United States at the time, as 1 million gallons of oil poured into the Kalamazoo River in Michigan from a broken pipeline in July 2010. These incidents remind us that the dangers of oil exploration and transportation are not limited to the deep ocean.

Campaigners say that many accidents are caused by cost cutting and poor maintenance. Maintenance is especially important in offshore equipment where the stresses from undersea pressure and extreme weather are often much greater. The campaigners argue that governments need to be stricter in making sure that safety standards are high.

European views

Feelings against offshore drilling in the United States are generally stronger than those held in the UK and Europe. Some people think this is because the rigs are not as close to the shoreline as they are in the United States. There is also the fact that the North Sea oil developments took place before environmental campaigning really became popular. In the United States, an oil well ruptured off the coast of California in 1969, causing hundreds of thousands of liters of oil to leak out. This was at a time when environmentalism was becoming popular. The disaster led to a ban on offshore drilling that lasted until 2008. There are calls now for it to be reinstated.

Regulating oil companies

The Deepwater Horizon disaster was not the first deep-sea incident but it convinced governments across the world that deep-sea drilling was very risky. As the disaster unfolded, the U.S. government stopped all new applications for deep-sea drilling licences. A commission was set up to see what lessons could be learned from the disaster.

■ Industries like fishing are badly affected when oil spills into the sea. Governments have to protect other people and businesses from problems caused by oil companies.

When an accident happens, governments can impose a large fine. A criminal investigation may also be ordered to see if any laws were broken. This can be very complex. A major deep-sea drilling project normally involves many different companies so it can be difficult to pinpoint who is responsible for an accident. In the Deepwater Horizon project, BP owned the oil well but other companies owned the rig and carried out key tasks like cementing the well. In the end, the company that operates the rig and will make most of the money from it is responsible.

The Deepwater Horizon disaster also exposed problems in the way safety rules were enforced. Safety inspections were often not being made. The U.S. government put in place a new agency to regulate the oil companies. They hope that this will make the oil industry safer.

It is "essential that going forward we put in place every necessary safeguard and protection so that a tragedy like this oil spill does not happen again.... I will not tolerate more finger-pointing or irresponsibility."

President Obama, speaking after the Deepwater Horizon disaster (Source: *Washington Post*, May 15, 2010)

Stopping the next disaster

Opponents argue that the oil industry is too powerful to be regulated effectively. Oil companies know that governments of countries that import a lot of oil, like the United States and United Kingdom, want to control more of their own oil needs by deep-sea oil drilling. If they impose too many restrictions, the oil companies will drill for oil in other countries.

For the oil companies, the cost of catastrophic accidents can be incredibly high. They argue that they will regulate themselves to prevent a spill like Deepwater Horizon from happening again. Several oil companies have already agreed to work together on a response system for oil spills in the Gulf of Mexico. Regulators and residents of the Gulf Coast wait to see if this will stop another disaster happening.

THE FUTURE FOR OFFSHORE DRILLING

Following the Deepwater Horizon disaster many countries had to weigh the risk of a major accident against the benefits of deepwater drilling. These countries also had to think about the risks of relying on imported oil from other countries or other sources of oil that might be even more controversial, like the Canadian tar sands.

Deeper and deeper?

Some countries stopped new drilling for a period of time. The world's thirst for oil will almost certainly mean that deepwater drilling will continue, even if there is strong opposition. New technologies will be developed so oil can be found in deeper and more remote seas, such as the Arctic, where drilling rigs and oil platforms will be faced with extreme cold and icebergs.

The amount of oil the world uses will also continue to rise unless we change the way we power our vehicles and generate power. This may be forced on us if oil becomes more difficult to produce, and the price of oil rises. The biggest risk of our reliance on oil is **global warming**. Major changes in climate and a rise in sea level would have much more impact than even the biggest oil spill.

Political issues

As well as safety and environmental issues, deepwater oil exploration will continue to cause political controversy. The United Kingdom and Argentina fought a war over who should control the Falkland Islands in 1982. There has been much speculation that this war was fought because of the potential oil reserves beneath the South Atlantic Ocean that surrounds the islands, although that was not the reason given at the time.

■ A small rise in sea level means that islands like the Maldives would disappear beneath the ocean.

DEBATE: ARE BIG OIL COMPANIES ONLY INTERESTED IN PROFITS?

Arguments for:

- The Deepwater Horizon is the biggest of thousands of accidents offshore and onshore. If companies cared about the environment they would try harder to reduce the impact of the oil industry.
- Oil companies have ignored all the evidence on climate change, putting huge amounts of money into finding more oil rather than supporting renewable energy or reducing the amount of oil we use.
- Oil companies have only improved safety and looked at their impact on the environment when they have been forced to by governments.

Arguments against:

- Oil companies need to look for new sources of oil. Making a profit does not mean they are unconcerned about safety. After all, the people who work for oil companies have families; they care about their own lives, the lives of others, and the environment.
- Finding oil beneath the ocean is difficult and dangerous, but oil is needed and sometimes accidents happen.
- Major oil accidents are extremely expensive as companies have to clean up the mess, pay money to the people affected, and pay fines. They also affect the reputation of the company. Companies that want to make profits do all they can to avoid disasters.

SOURCES OF ENERGY

Non-renewable alternatives to deep-sea oil exploration

Fuel	Easy to access?	Positives	Environmental impact	Other major drawbacks
Oil – offshore	No – most stocks in deep ocean, limited supply	Extremely versatile fuel. Accessible reserves close to countries that do not have onshore oil.	Use in vehicles is major contributor to climate change. Use in plastics that do not decay (not biodegradable).	Risks of major damage from ruptured oil wells or undersea pipelines
Oil – onshore	Getting less easy – large reserves in Middle East but some reserves are running dry	Still cheapest and easiest oil to access	Use in vehicles is major contributor to climate change	Main importing countries have low reserves so need to import
Oil – tar sands	No – needs large input of energy to be usable as oil	Large reserves remaining in stable countries (e.g. Canada)	Double release of greenhouse gases. Huge mining operation.	Potential for accidents when transporting by sea or pipeline
Gas	Yes – large reserves remaining	Cleaner than oil. Less risk of pollution when extracting. Can be used in vehicles.	Releases greenhouse gases (although fewer than oil or coal)	Potential for accidents when transporting by sea or pipeline
Coal	Yes – large reserves remaining	Easy and cheap to mine. Can be broken down to reduce carbon emissions when burned.	Biggest source of greenhouse gases	Difficult to transport. Major reserves concentrated in few countries, some of which are unstable.
Nuclear (current fuel is non-renewable)	Fuel is accessible but building reactors to get energy from it is very expensive	No carbon emissions. Fuel is plentiful at present.	Problems of disposing of used fuel, which remains hazardous for hundreds of years	Much less versatile than oil or gas. Difficult and dangerous conditions for workers.

Renewable alternatives to deep-sea oil exploration

Fuel	Easy to access?	Positives	Environmental impact	Other major drawbacks
Biofuels	Yes – can be grown widely	Versatile. Can be combined with oil to power vehicles. Absorbs carbon while growing.	Carbon emissions when burnt	Uses agricultural land needed for food. Would require huge areas to be grown to replace oil.
Solar	Yes – capturing the Sun's energy	Totally clean and renewable. No carbon emissions.	Huge areas of solar panels needed to capture the Sun's energy	Not so effective in cooler (and cloudier) climates
Wind	Yes	Clean and renewable. No carbon emissions.	Wind turbines are noisy and ugly. Can be dangerous for birds.	Only effective in certain places and power cannot be generated all the time. Huge areas of turbines needed to generate enough power.
Hydro-electric (using rivers and dams)	Yes, but often in isolated areas	Clean and renewable. No carbon emissions.	Building dams on rivers floods valleys and changes habitats	Mainly available in mountainous or coastal areas. Power needs long lines to reach population centres.
Wave and tidal	Plentiful but difficult and expensive to harness	Clean and renewable. No carbon emissions.	Tidal barrages can damage ecosystems	Initial costs are very high
Geothermal energy (using heat beneath Earth's crust to turn water to steam and drive turbines)	Not possible in all areas	Clean and renewable, without some of the drawbacks of wind and solar energy	Minimal	Only possible in some areas

GLOSSARY

ally a country connected to another by an agreement or treaty

barrel oil is measured in barrels. A barrel of oil is 42 gallons or 159 liters.

blowout when gas or oil rushes out of an oil well without being controlled

carbon dioxide (CO$_2$) gas that is emitted when plants and animals breathe and when products containing carbon, including oil, are burned in air. Most scientists think that increased CO$_2$ in the atmosphere is responsible for Earth's climate getting warmer.

contaminate become polluted or poisoned

continental shelf sloping area of seabed between the edge of a continent and deep ocean

crude oil form oil takes when it is extracted from the ground. Crude oil needs to be refined to make useful products.

descendant person coming directly from an earlier and usually similar individual

developing country poorer country where the economy is not yet fully developed. Examples include many countries in Africa, Asia, and South America.

dispersant chemical that is used to break up oil in the sea

distillation separating materials that have different boiling points by boiling off different substances. Distillation is one method used in the refining of crude oil.

drill string lengths of interlocking pipe connecting a drilling rig to the drill bit that is boring an oil well

ecosystem environment and the plants and animals it contains

emissions something discharged

environmentalist someone who campaigns to prevent damage to the environment

export goods that are sold to other countries

fossil fuels also called hydrocarbons. They are made up of molecules that contain hydrogen and carbon. When they are burned, energy is released, depending on how much hydrogen is in the compound.

geologist scientist who studies earth history and life especially as recorded in rock

global warming widely accepted theory that Earth's climate is getting warmer because of the actions of humans (such as burning fossil fuels)

greenhouse gases gases including carbon dioxide that cause climate change

import goods that are bought from another country, such as oil imported from Saudi Arabia

marine of the sea, such as marine animals that live in the sea

micro-organism tiny living things such as bacteria and viruses that can only be seen with a microscope

non-renewable resources, like oil, that once used, cannot be replaced

oil well hole in the ground or seabed that is drilled to access oil

OPEC (Organization of Petroleum Exporting Countries) group of countries, many in the Middle East, that control much of the world's oil reserves and production

petrochemical substance obtained from crude oil that can be used to make other products such as plastics

poverty lack of money or possessions

pressure (air and water) the force applied by air and water. This varies depending on where we are. Air pressure is lower above sea level and water pressure increases with depth.

refinery industrial plant where crude oil is turned into various products, including gasoline and petrochemicals

renewable resources that can be replaced, or grown again

reserves oil that has been discovered but not yet extracted from under the ground

sedimentary rock rock formed by layers of sand or mud over millions of years

seismic relating to Earth's crust

sonar instrument for detecting the presence and location of submerged objects by sound waves

survey to find out the size, shape, and position of (as an area of land)

thruster jet or propeller on an offshore rig that is used for maintaining the rig's position

valve device for controlling flow of liquid or gas through a pipe. Valves may only allow liquids to flow in one direction.

wetlands area of land that is covered in shallow water, such as a swamp or marsh

FURTHER INFORMATION

Books

Calvert, John. *The Arabian Peninsula in the Age of Oil* (Making of the Middle East). Broomall, PA: Mason Crest, 2007.

Coad, John. *Finding and Using Oil* (Why Science Matters). Chicago, IL: Heinemann Library, 2008.

Doeden, Matt, *Green Energy* (USA TODAY's Debate: Voices and Perspectives), 21st Century Books, Minneapolis, 2010.

Hartman, Eve and Wendy Meshbesher, *Searching for Arctic Oil* (Science Missions). Chicago, IL: Raintree Publishers, 2010.

Jovinelly, Joann. *Oil: The Economics of Fuel* (In the News). New York: Rosen Publishing, 2008.

Lewandowski, Laura Christine. *Goodbye Gasoline* (Headline Science). Mankato, MN: Compass Point Books, 2007.

Websites

The Deepwater Horizon disaster led to lots of coverage of oil and deep-sea drilling by many major news organizations.

The *New York Times* has a section devoted to oil at **topics.nytimes.com/top/ news/business/energy-environment/oil-petroleum-and-gasoline/ index.html**

The BBC has a section that pulls together all its coverage of the Deepwater Horizon spill at **www.bbc.co.uk/news/special_reports/oil_disaster/**

The US National Oceanic and Atmospheric Administration (NOAA) includes fascinating features about ocean life and also has a section on the Deepwater Horizon oil spill at **www.noaa.gov.**

Oil companies have their own websites that give details of their activities and policies on issues like climate change. Examples include **www.exxonmobil.com**, **www.bp.com**, **www.shell.com**

To get both sides of the argument, you should also look at the websites of environmental groups like **www.greenpeace.org**

Topics for further research

- Deepwater Horizon Disaster: The full impact of this disaster will not be known for a long time. How will it affect habitats and animal life? Will the fishing industry in the Gulf of Mexico recover? Will deep-sea drilling continue in the Gulf of Mexico?
- Climate change: This book looks briefly at the impact that burning oil and other fossil fuels is having on our climate. You can find out more about this topic and its possible impact in the years to come. Also look at the arguments of those who say that people are not causing climate change.

WORLD ENERGY SUPPLY

This table shows how far renewable energy has to go before it breaks the dominance of fossil fuels.

Fuel	% of world energy supply (2008)
Oil	33.2
Coal	27
Gas	21.1
Nuclear	5.8
Hydro-electricity	2.2
Biofuels, waste and combustible renewables	10
Other (including wind, solar, geothermal)	0.7

Source: International Energy Agency

INDEX